Jam

MW00883939

The Inspirational Story of Basketball Superstar James Harden

presentation of the information is without contract or any type of guarantee assurance.

The trademarks that are used are without any consent, and the publication of the trademark is without permission or backing by the trademark owner. All trademarks and brands within this book are for clarifying purposes only and are the owned by the owners themselves, not affiliated with this document.

Table Of Contents

Introduction

As the title already implies, this is a book about [The Inspirational Story of Basketball Superstar James Harden] and how he rose from his life in Compton, Los Angeles to becoming one of today's leading and most-respected basketball players. In his rise to superstardom, James has inspired not only the youth, but fans of all ages throughout the world.

This book also portrays the struggles that James has had to overcome during his early childhood years, his teen years, and up until he became what he is today. A notable source of inspiration is James' service to the community and his strong connection with the fans of the sport. He continues to serve as a humble, fun-loving superstar in a sport that glorifies flashy plays and mega personalities.

Combining a deadly step-back, incredible footwork, a feathery jump-shot, and high basketball IQ, James has shown the ability to completely take over a game. From being a young phenom to becoming one of the greatest guards of his generation, you'll learn here how this man has risen to the ranks of the best basketball players today.

Thanks again for downloading this book. Hopefully you can take some of the examples from James' story and apply them to your own life!

Chapter 1:

Youth & Family Life

The world welcomed James Edwards Harden, Jr. on August 26th, 1989. He was born in Los Angeles, California to father James Harden Sr. and mother Monja Willis. At the time of young James' birth, his father was enrolled in the United States Navy but later found his way down a path of drugs and multiple stints in jail. Because of this, James grew to rely on his mother and didn't have much association with his absentee father, later dropping the Jr. from his name.

James' mother, Monja, was a rock solid foundation for her son and she held a job as an administrator for the AT&T office located in Pasadena, California. James was the third child of his family but was more than ten years younger than his two siblings. His half-brother, Akili Roberson, was a very impressive quarterback for local Locke High School. He went on to play for the University of Kansas and was inspirational to young James.

James grew up in the Compton area of Los Angeles, specifically in the Rancho Dominguez locality - an area that has produced many talented athletes over the years. James was like his older brother Akili, in that he possessed natural athleticism to go along with above-average height. He was drawn to basketball, as many youngsters in the Southern California area are, and was lucky to have very good competition around him as he was growing up.

An obstacle that James had to overcome during his youth was that he suffered from the medical condition of asthma. He learned to accommodate his medical needs with an inhaler and did not let it affect how hard he played out on the court. Aside from being a solid student, James also enjoyed playing video games and watching basketball on television. He was a fan of UCLA basketball specifically, a college basketball powerhouse that was not far from his home.

Rancho Dominguez was not as dangerous as some other parts of Compton, but it was certainly not a safe area. There was a still a high number of property thefts and car/house break-ins when James was growing up. Because of this, Monja decided to send James outside the neighborhood for his education. James would enroll in Artesia High School in Lakewood, a suburb about fifteen minutes away from Rancho Dominguez. Monja looked out for her children and it ended up paying dividends for James and the family's future.

Not only was Artesia a well-respected school in the area, but it also featured one of the best basketball programs in Southern California. The school had developed a reputation for producing talented players such as Tom Tolbert and Jason Kapono, among others. The varsity coach, Scott Pera, was a top-tier high school coach who possessed a talent in developing raw players.

James would make the starting line-up of the varsity team as a sophomore and was able to average double digits in scoring. Artesia won almost thirty games during the season and showed great potential for the future. Between his sophomore and junior year, James hit a growth spurt and he noticeably improved his jump shot in the off-season. By the time his junior season started, Coach Pera was looking for James to have a more pronounced role in the team's offense.

A naturally unselfish player, James did not want to step on any toes and had to be encouraged to play aggressively at times. However, the players on the team believed in James' abilities and most importantly, Coach Pera saw and harnessed James' playmaking talents so that they could mutually benefit.

James responded by leading the Pioneers to the State Championship and a 33-1 record. He personally averaged almost 20 points per game and his ability to take over in the clutch was beginning to develop. He would use this momentum and confidence boost to further develop his game in the AAU circuit, becoming an all-around player who could score upwards of twenty points in a game, as well as lock down an opposing player for stretches at a time.

Towards the end of the summer, James had a statement game in Las Vegas, when he scored almost 70 points in back-to-back games. Not only did he accomplish such a difficult feat, but the opposing teams had big name studs such as Kevin Love, Michael Beasley, Austin Freeman, and Nolan Smith.

Coming into his senior season with high expectations and his confidence at an all-time high, James was able to lead his team to another state championship, this time under coach Loren Grover. They won 33 games once again and James showed true comfort as the star player for the team. Arguably just as important, James was able to help nurture burgeoning stars Renardo Sidney and Malik Story, who were both younger than James. His leadership put Artesia in a position to stay at the top even after he would leave.

During his youth, James looked up to San Antonio Spurs star guard, Manu Ginobili. As both were left-handed nifty players, James tried to implement many of Manu's moves into his own repertoire. As he began to develop into his own, scouts and coaches noted that James' basketball IQ was very impressive for his age.

Chapter 2:

College

Because James had such a decorated high school and AAU career, he had some leverage with his multitude of scholarship offers. With Monja moving to Phoenix because her mother had just passed away and left her a home in her will, along with his former coach and mentor, Scott Pera, now working as an assistant, Arizona State University was the clear-cut favorite in James' mind.

Even with James' arrival, the Arizona State Sun Devils were not seriously considered to be more than a .500 team in the competitive Pac-10. James would be counted on to lead the team to new heights and he was ready to embrace that role. He would go on to lead the team to an overall record of 21-13, along with point guard Derek Glasser and forward Ty Pendergraph. Statistically, James led the team with almost an eighteen points per game average to go along with more than two steals per game. His three-point percentage was over 40% making him a deadly shooter by college basketball standards.

Surprising to most around the country, the Sun Devils were in consideration for the NCAA Tournament by the end of the regular season. Despite the fact that they slightly missed one of the last tournament spots, Arizona State was still able to make some noise in the NIT Tournament and well exceeded the outside expectations put on them. For James, he finished his freshman campaign being named to the First-Team All Pac-10 team and was a no-brainer for the conference All-Freshman Team.

By the beginning of his sophomore season, James had grown into a celebrity on campus, as many of the students would wear memorabilia sporting phrases about James - including shirts that read, "Die Harden Fan". Tempe was embracing James and he would use the momentum to his advantage. In a game against UTEP, James dropped forty points and completely took over the game. This performance also placed James into consideration as one of the best scorers in the entire conference. He finished the season with an average of over twenty points per game and led the Pac-10 in total steals for the second consecutive season.

As a sign of recognition, James was voted as the Pac-10 Player of the Year and was given national attention by the media and even the underground college basketball fans. He was even named a consensus All-American. For the season, ASU won twenty games and were able to make it into the NCAA Tournament as a sixth seed, but lost in the second round to third seeded powerhouse, Syracuse.

After the college basketball season ended, it became apparent that James had potential to play in the NBA and he seized the opportunity. He would declare for the NBA Draft after only his sophomore season. To help him in his guidance and negotiations, James decided to go with accomplished agent Rob Pelinka.

Chapter 3:

Professional Life

First Season

As there was little doubt that Oklahoma's Blake Griffin would be selected with the number one overall pick by the Los Angeles Clippers, James was hoping that he would follow soon after. The Oklahoma City Thunder were very impressed by James' maturity and skill set, and General Manager Sam Presti decided that James was their guy. With the number three pick in the draft, James was chosen by the Thunder as the first player to be drafted by the franchise since its move from Seattle.

The franchise was still in rebuilding mode after drafting talented players like Russell Westbrook, Kevin Durant and Jeff Green and hoped that James could become another piece in the rebuilding process. The team had only won 23 games in the previous season and there was not much outside expectations for the team to make the playoffs in the loaded Western Conference.

James was given more than twenty minutes per game as a rookie, showing that he could be an integral part of the Thunder's rotation. In this limited amount of playing time, James was still able to average around ten points per game and was named to the NBA All-Rookie Second Team. His role as the sixth man of the team allowed James to provide instant-offense off the bench for a team that desperately needed scoring while its starters were resting.

The team finished the regular season with a surprising fifty win total and was able to make the Western Conference Playoffs. They faced the Los Angeles Lakers in the first round and came up short, but they were competitive in almost every game in the series. James was able to really show promise as a scorer and defender during the highly anticipated series. He scored eighteen points in Game 3 and had a couple of steals in Game 4.

Second Season

James entered his second season with a feeling of belonging and the team designated him as one of the key pieces moving forward. He played in every regular season game and averaged more than twelve points per game. He would play even better in the Playoffs than he did in the regular season, as he raised his scoring average to thirteen points per game and shot almost 50% from the field.

James was also starting to develop a reputation as more than just a scorer, he was a play-maker. A play-maker is a rarity on the NBA level. The big difference between a scorer and a play-maker is that a play-maker can get his own shot but also has the awareness and ability to make the other players on the court better by creating opportunities for them.

James' three point shooting really opened up the floor and spread defenses thin when they played against the three-headed monster of a Durant-Westbrook-Harden line-up. The team would win 55 games for the season and grab first place of the Northwest Division, surpassing outside expectations once again - a trend you probably have noticed now for teams that James plays on. In the playoffs, the Thunder would make it all the way to the Western Conference Finals, beating the Denver Nuggets and Memphis Grizzlies along the way.

After meeting the red-hot Dallas Mavericks in the Conference Finals, Dirk Nowitzki and company were a little too much for the inexperienced Thunder, as they took ahold of the pace and controlled the tempo of the series, even though all five games were close.

Third Season

Despite their young core, the Thunder entered the 2011-12 season as one of the favorites to contend for a championship. Their star players were still well below their prime and the fan base felt optimistic in Oklahoma City.

The team would go on to win the Northwest Division once again and James took his role as the Sixth Man to another level. He had multiple offensive explosions during the season, including a 40 point game against the Phoenix Suns. He was able to score over twenty points in fourteen different games and had three games of more than thirty points. Furthermore, he was getting these points in a very efficient manner. Not only was he only playing a little over thirty minutes a game, but James was also second in the entire NBA in true shooting percentage and effective field goal percentage.

This display of dominance led James to being named the NBA's Sixth Man of the Year and put him among the top fifteen or so scorers in the entire league. James was also the second youngest player to ever win the award, showing that he could probably take on a bigger role for the team. As most players who win the award are in their prime or on the back end of their career, rarely does a man in his first few seasons win it.

Because of a setback from an elbow to the head by Metta World Peace, James was forced to miss a number of games because of a concussion. However, he returned for the Playoffs and picked up right where he left off. The Thunder entered the first round in a rematch against the Dallas Mavericks, this time sweeping Dallas handily. James showed that he had superstar potential when he came through in the biggest game of the series, scoring 29 points in Game 4.

From there, the Thunder beat the Los Angeles Lakers and James showed defensive brilliance as he was assigned to guard Kobe Bryant in clutch moments of the series. He had eight steals in only five games. After Oklahoma City beat the Lakers in five games, they met the well-respected San Antonio Spurs in the Western Conference Finals.

The Thunder were able to harness their youth and naivete into a four game winning streak after being dominated in the first two games of the series. James would score twenty points in the Game 5 victory and hit multiple clutch baskets. This series victory would earn the Thunder a berth into the NBA Finals to play against the Miami Heat.

The favorite, Miami Heat, would beat the Thunder in relatively easy fashion but the Thunder had taken another big step forward as a franchise, finally winning their conference. The future looked bright in Oklahoma City and the fan base couldn't have been any more proud of the effort put forth by the squad.

As a surprise to many around the league, James was asked to join teammates Russell Westbrook and Kevin Durant on the 2012 Olympic Team as one of the last players added to the roster. This served notice that James was considered to be one of the elite players in the game and that he was on the same level as the guys he went to London with. The team would go on to be undefeated in the Olympics and brought a Gold Medal back home to the United States.

Fourth Season

Just before the 2012-13 season kicked off, the Thunder were looking to make a deal with James for a contract extension and a secured role as the sixth man for the team. However, James believed that he could provide a bigger role and the Thunder worked out a trade with the Houston Rockets. This show of faith and confidence would lead James into a position that he would be grateful for. This foresight was questioned by many around the league, but James did not disappoint.

Daryl Morey, the Rockets general manager, showed confidence in James by calling him a "foundational player" for the team's future. After signing a max-level contract with the Rockets soon after arriving, James turned into a straight up stud. His abilities were on display instantly, as his first game posted statistics including 37 points, 12 assists, 6 rebounds, and 4 steals.

His first performance as a Rocket put him into legendary company as the only player in franchise history to tie Hakeem Olajuwon's stat-line of 37/12. He would go on to score 45 points in his second game for a combined 82 in his first two games - a historic start for any player still adjusting to a new team. His play during the first week of the season would garner him the Western Conference Player of the Week award.

James would continue this momentum and post games of 40-plus points as well as a few double-digit assist games. Most importantly, he provided the organization with a go-to player who could take over a game and lead the young core around him. James would go on to win another Player of the Week award and even had a streak of scoring 25 points in fourteen straight games - a franchise record.

This rise to superstardom, gave James a position on the Western Conference All-Star Team and he even scored fifteen points in the game. After the All-Star Break, James would go on to set a career-high of 46 points against his former team, the Oklahoma City Thunder.

The season served as a coming-out party for James and showed many doubters around the league that he made the right decision to ask for a bigger role in his occupation. He was a superstar talent that deserved a superstar role, and the Rockets sure were glad about that. His season average of almost 26 points per game and almost 2 steals per game were both career highs.

The team would eventually make the playoffs as the eighth seed but did not make it past the first round matchup against the Oklahoma City Thunder. However, James and the Rockets were able to win two games in the series and he performed admirably despite having flu-like symptoms in the last two games of the series. His postseason averages of more than 26 points, almost 7 rebounds, 5 assists, and two steals, were playoff career highs for him.

His 2012-13 campaign earned him All-NBA Third Team honors and placed him in the conversation among the best shooting guards in the NBA.

Fifth Season

After signing center Dwight Howard in free agency, Rockets management felt like they could begin pushing to create one of the best rosters in the league. Dwight and James became one of the best duos in the game and the best guard-center offensive combination.

The team greatly improved from the previous season, winning 54 games and earning the fifth seed in the Western Conference Playoffs. The team would eventually lose to the Portland Trail

Blazers in a closely fought series, but the future was bright in Houston and the Rockets could only improve as their duo became more comfortable with each other.

James was recognized as one of the best players in the game when he was named to the 2014 All-NBA First Team, a very sought after accomplishment by players around the league.

Chapter 4:

Personal Adult Life

James has developed a well-rounded character and has a like-able personality both on and off the court. He serves as one of the more intriguing stars in the league because of his fashion sense, iconic beard, and marketable personality. James has appeared in a number of commercials, including ones for Foot Locker and BBVA. His sense of humor shines through when he gives interviews and his stoic expressions always make for a great laugh.

James has publicly stated that he is a Christian. He has talked about his faith, saying things like he wants to "thank God for everything he has done" in his life. Throughout all of the struggles that James has had to overcome during his childhood and youth, he has been able to put his family into a position of success and abundance. This could have only been accomplished through staying humble and a confidence that could not be broken.

As for James' iconic beard, he started growing it during his college days because he was too lazy to shave. He maintained a relatively shorter beard during college and even in the beginning of his professional career, but later went all-out with the full, sculpted look to go along with the mo-hawk. This appearance is one of the most memorable amongst casual fans and James has developed his own "look", something that a lot of men wish they could achieve.

Throughout his rise to stardom, fans have become creative, making t-shirts, fake beards, and posters to show their support for James. Seeing phrases like "Fear the Beard" are common at any Houston Rockets home game.

Chapter 5:

Philanthropic/Charitable Acts

Throughout James' stops in his short time as a professional, he has made sure to give back to the communities that support him - whether it be Oklahoma City, Houston, or his hometown of Los Angeles.

Recently, alongside teammate Jeremy Lin, James participated in a shopping spree for select children from disadvantaged families. The spree was funded by James and was done in the name of the holiday spirit. James participated in this with his mother, Monja, and it made a huge impact in the lives of the selected families. Not only was the financial help appreciated, but the action was very generous and it gave hope to the children who were affected by it.

Chapter 6:

Legacy, Potential & Inspiration

James' career is still young but we can learn much from his journey. Not only is he a prime example of succeeding despite being from a single parent household, he also shows us that believing in yourself can go a long way.

Whether it was giving himself permission to be a little more selfish at Artesia High, deciding to trust in himself in a superstar role, or even growing a beard that other people might view as "weird", James' confidence shines through. His belief in his own abilities allows other teammates to trust him with the ball, knowing that he will eventually make the right decision most of the time. Because of this, they find themselves with open shots and easy looks based on his penetration and court vision.

The future in Houston remains to be seen, but what is certain is that James is one of those generational players who is bigger than basketball. His persona brings fans into the stadium and buying his jersey. He is the type of star player that general managers dream of and a son that his mother, Monja, has become extremely proud of.

With the aging Dwyane Wade and Kobe Bryant, the NBA is looking to hand James the torch as the premier shooting guard in the league. While James is still quite young and there are still other promising shooting guards such as Demar DeRozan and Klay Thompson, James has shown that his work ethic and basketball IQ will always keep him relevant and at the top - much like one of his childhood role models, Manu Ginobili.

Chapter 7:

Notable Statistics & Career Milestones

Here is a list of accomplishments that James has achieved in his young career so far:

- NBA All-Star (2013, 2014)

- All-NBA First Team (2014)

- All-NBA Third Team (2013)

- NBA Sixth Man of the Year (2012)

- NBA All-Rookie Second Team (2010)

- Pac-10 Player of the Year (2009)

- First-Team All-American (2009)

Conclusion

I hope this book was able to help you gain inspiration from the life of James Harden, one of the best players currently playing in the National Basketball Association.

The rise and fall of a star is often the cause for much wonder. But most stars have an expiration date. In basketball, once a star player reaches his mid- to late-thirties, it is often time to contemplate retirement. What will be left in people's minds about that fading star? In James' case, people will remember how he led a franchise in their journey towards a championship. He will be remembered as the guy who plucked his franchise from obscurity, helped them build their image, and honed his own image along the way.

James has also inspired so many people because he is the star who never fails to connect with fans and give back to the less fortunate. Noted for his ability to impose his will on any game, he is a joy to watch on the basketball court. Last but not least, he's remarkable for remaining simple and firm with his principles in spite of his immense popularity.

Hopefully you learned some great things about James in this book and are able to apply some of the lessons that you've learned to your own life! Good luck in your own journey!

Other Basketball Stories That Will Inspire You!

Kevin Durant

http://www.amazon.com/dp/B00HIKDK34

Stephen Curry

http://www.amazon.com/dp/B00HH9QU1A

Derrick Rose

http://www.amazon.com/dp/B00HH1BE82

Blake Griffin

http://www.amazon.com/dp/B00INNVVIG

Carmelo Anthony

http://www.amazon.com/dp/B00HH9L3P8

Chris Paul

http://www.amazon.com/dp/B00HIZXMSW

Paul George

http://www.amazon.com/dp/B00IN3YIVI

Dirk Nowitzki

http://www.amazon.com/dp/B00HRVPD9I

Inspirational Football Stories!

Peyton Manning

http://www.amazon.com/dp/B00HJUYTCY

Tom Brady

http://www.amazon.com/dp/B00HJYQTRS

Aaron Rodgers

http://www.amazon.com/dp/B00HJUEDEI

Colin Kaepernick

http://www.amazon.com/dp/B00IRHHABU

Russell Wilson

http://www.amazon.com/dp/B00HK909C8

Calvin Johnson

http://www.amazon.com/dp/B00HJK0YS2

Other Inspirational Stories!

Mike Trout

http://www.amazon.com/dp/B00HKKCNNU

Miguel Cabrera

http://www.amazon.com/dp/B00HKG3G1W

Buster Posey

http://www.amazon.com/dp/B00KP11V9S

Lou Gehrig

http://www.amazon.com/dp/B00KOZMONW

Babe Ruth

http://www.amazon.com/dp/B00IS2YB48

Floyd Mayweather

http://www.amazon.com/dp/B00HLEX5O6

Anderson Silva

http://www.amazon.com/dp/BooHLBOVVU

Made in the USA
Lexington, KY
24 July 2015